PRAISE
The Smooth Traveler: Avoiding Cross-Cultural Mistakes at Home

CW00500156

Sue O'Halloran's book on common cross-cultural mistakes brings the whole issue of cultural sensitivity to the forefront with specific examples from the U.S. and around the globe. Sue provides practical, simple guidelines that can be applied to any cross-cultural situation in your family, business or community. Her advice is seasoned by her consistent engagement with the issue.

Salim Muwakkil, Senior Editor of *In These Times* and host of the Salim Muwakkil Show, WVON-AM

• • •

Susan O'Halloran provides exactly what many people are seeking: ways to be respectful and value differences, rather than pretend they don't exist! In our racial equity work at the YWCA, we often say that eliminating racism happens one conversation at a time, and Sue's wonderful book gives readers the tools to enter cross-cultural dialogues or situations with confidence.

Karen Singer, President and CEO, YWCA Evanston/North Shore

• • •

The Smooth Traveler: Avoiding Cross-Cultural Mistakes at Home and Abroad *is welcome relief to the race-baiting and other hate language that proliferates our media today. Susan O'Halloran's common sense approach brings large issues down to size and highlights ordinary people who care to be kind to one another. Most people want to behave well and this book delivers the awareness and skills to go beyond our good intentions.*

Ray Hanania, Managing Editor *The Arab Daily News*

Susan O'Halloran provides a great starting place for those dipping their toe into cross-cultural conversations and travel.

Crystal Chan, author of *Bird* and speaker on mixed-race diversity

• • •

Susan O'Halloran's book, The Smooth Traveler: Avoiding Cross-Cultural Mistakes at Home and Abroad *is a fresh approach for all of us as it focuses on how to live in our world of diversity and conflicting thoughts. The book in a simple way educates us in how to share and care for each other for a better world. This book gives the skills of negotiating those differences and resolving conflicts should they arise.*

Dr. Osman Ahmed, Ph.D., P.E.
Past President, Member of Majlis-e-Shura

Susan O'Halloran

THE SMOOTH TRAVELER

Avoiding Cross-Cultural Mistakes at Home and Abroad

Visit Susan O'Halloran at www.susanohalloran.com

The Smooth Traveler: Avoiding Cross-Cultural Mistakes at Home and Abroad
Copyright © 2016 Susan O'Halloran. All rights reserved.
Evanston, Illinois

Library of Congress Cataloguing-in-Publication Data

O'Halloran, Susan 1/15/16
The Smooth Traveler: Avoiding Cross-Cultural Mistakes at Home and Abroad / Susan O'Halloran
        87 pages cm

ISBN-10:1530666023
ISBN-13: 978-1530666027

1. Educational curriculum   2. Diversity and Inclusion

Printed in the United States of America
createspace.com

TABLE OF CONTENTS

INTRODUCTION

Before my first trip overseas, a friend from Europe said to me, "Don't be one of those Americans who expects to find the U.S. everywhere you go. Don't think everything should be as you find it at home and everyone should be marching to America's tune." In other words, he was telling me don't be "rude," "arrogant," "impatient" and "thoughtless" - the stereotype of the "Ugly American."

I think there is a greater awareness today that, if you are going to travel abroad, it's a good idea to take the time to learn some of the language, history, customs and traditions of the countries you will visit. However, you don't need to travel the world to experience the world. It's all right here in the United States. You don't have to leave your hometown to experience other cultures:

- Someone in your family has married a Korean, Australian, Irish or Turkish partner. Now, you are spending the holidays with that side of the family - what do you say? How do you act?

- A colleague at work who is from Spain or Ghana or Jordan invites you to his son's wedding. What do you wear? What kind of gift should you give? What should you expect?

- Or, perhaps, you are going to travel to a different part of the U.S. You are going to encounter people from an American culture you have little experience with such as the Amish or Polish Americans or Lakota or Southerners or Northerners or Californians or ranchers or young urban professionals... on and on.

Without meaning to be, you could be an "Ugly American" right here in the United States.

This book is designed to give you greater awareness of the type and variety of differences you may encounter plus skill in negotiating those diversities and in repairing relationships if conflicts occur.

Not only will you gain greater appreciation for other people's depth and intricacies, I hope you will come to value all the large hopes and small miracles that created you.

Susan O'Halloran

www.SusanOHalloran
susan@susanohalloran.com
1-866-997-8726

PART ONE: WHAT IS CULTURE?

WE ARE ALL MULTI-CULTURAL

Culture is a shared design for living. You can think of this idea of culture pretty easily when you think of people's ethnic or national backgrounds. No matter how disguised, ignored, or blended through marriage and time, the fact remains that your ethnic background can give you a great deal of strength, pride and identity.

However, the definition of culture goes beyond your ethnic background to include other dimensions of diversity such as geography, gender, language, physical abilities, work experience, religious beliefs, educational background and so on.

You may have experienced these categories as cultures if, for example, your family changed from living a military to a civilian life. That's a *real* culture shock for many. Or, perhaps, you moved from one part of this country to another to go to school. If you moved from rural Omaha to New York City, for example, your whole relationship to time and space could change. In New York City everything moves faster. More often you find yourself looking up rather than looking out onto wide-open spaces. Each region of the country has a distinct feel and set of expectations and, therefore, can seem like a whole different culture.

THE SCRIPTS YOU LIVE BY

Each of your cultures gave you a "script" to live by. When an actor stars in a movie, he or she is handed a script. The script tells the actors what to say and the stage directions tell the actors what to do. The script literally tells the actors who they are and what role they are playing.

As you grew up, people in your cultures were handing you scripts as well.

How many of you chose your first school or your first church, temple, mosque or synagogue? How many of you looked up at your parents, a babe in arm, and said, "Mom or Dad, I want to live in *this* neighborhood?" No. Your parents or guardians made those choices for you. That was their job.

With each choice your parents or caretakers made for you, you entered into a specific culture. It's as if each of us landed on a different Hollywood set. Some of us grew up on sets that could only be described as sitcoms. Some of us have been trapped in high drama. For some, you could only call the scripts you were handed Science Fiction. Your experience of life so far has simply been unearthly, Sci-Fi bizarre!

Each of these cultures, because they share a design for living, handed you scripts so that you could make sense of the world. Hundreds of these scripts make up a culture's worldview. Each culture says, "This is how we do things here and here are your lines so that you can fit in. This is the role you'll play."

Sometimes these scripts are conscious; often they are not. I call these scripts unconscious or unspoken because you, for example, may not have been blatantly instructed to shake your head up and down to mean "yes". If that's the way your culture signals agreement, no one had to tell you in so many words what shaking your head up and down means. Growing up, you imitated the gestures and speaking styles around you. You absorbed the customs and rituals of the adults who raised you.

When you are born and raised in a culture, you know how to act within that culture. You know your role and what's expected of you.

But what happens when you travel outside your culture?

NO RULEBOOK

What happens is you make mistakes.

You don't mean to be rude or insensitive or insulting, but you don't have the rulebook. Families, neighborhoods, schools, workplaces, religious institutions - all of us - are experiencing an unprecedented mixing of cultures from around the world and from around the United States. It is understandable that many of us are asking for the rules.

You may request, "Just tell me what to say or what *not* to say or do around each group."

Of course, dealing with human beings is never that simple.

YOU ARE PART OF AND DISTINCT FROM YOUR CULTURES

The Dutch psychologist, Geert Hofstede, created a huge database of the ways cultures differ from one another. He developed a number of scales (now referred to as "Hofstede's Dimensions") that measure differences - such as the difference between persons or groups when it comes to individualism versus collectivism or the ability to tolerate ambiguity in contrast to the desire to avoid uncertainty.

First of all, there was no right or wrong to where any one group landed on his scales. Secondly, understanding a culture's position on any one of these dimensions *could never predict where any one individual might settle.*

That's why there is no cultural rulebook. Groups do share similar characteristics because of common experiences of geography, history, and the like. We can speak of the ways French people are different from Americans, the way Americans are different from Japanese people, and so on.

However, we always want to remember that groups of people only have *a tendency* toward sameness. No member of any group is like everyone else in that group. Think how impossible it would be for all men, all women, all New Yorkers, all Southerners, all dogs, all cats, all of *anything* to be the same.

You can't help but see similarities within certain groups of people and, at the same time, you need to be ready to see and treat people as individuals.

Isn't that how most of us want to be treated? You don't mind that people see that you have things in common with other people your age, for example, but you probably cringe when you hear someone say, "All (name your age group) are..."

Most people want to be treated as individuals as well as members of their groups. We need to move from the false security of categorizing people to the reality that people are much more complex and interesting than any one label can suggest.

EVER-FLUID CULTURES

People fit along a continuum of similarities and differences, and it's best that you know where any individual with whom you are studying, working, visiting or loving places him or herself. Holding the "Both/And" of cultures - we are *both* similar *and* we are different from the groups to which we belong - has immediate and practical benefits.

For example, the Chinese culture in general may be more concerned with group achievement than individual recognition, but that may not be true of your web designer who is Chinese. She *loves* praise and attention. Good to know, yes?

Sometimes in an effort to become familiar with a group's characteristics, we wind up re-stereotyping that group, albeit with more sophisticated over-generalizations.

In addition, as you learn cross-cultural skills, keep in mind that cultures are never static. They are constantly changing. Every culture has inconsistent values and a mixture of influences that are hard to grasp when part of that culture, let alone when looking at it from the outside.

In the same respect, people who have lived abroad - those who have come to the U.S. from another country or American expatriates living in other parts of the world - talk about being viewed as outsiders when they return home.

Some individuals so absorb their adopted country's customs that they almost forget how they were before they were immersed in another culture. It's never as easy as saying, "He's from such and such group, therefore x, y, and z."

You can't pigeonhole others or yourself. Be ready to be a surprise to yourself and to be surprised by others. You are going to find unexpected connections with people who seem very different from you. We are all multi-cultural and each culture has a wide spectrum of interests, personalities, and gifts to offer.

THINK IN TERMS OF CONTINUUMS

Rather than learning that someone is Mexican American or a Western cowhand or a Muslim or a Navy SEAL and turning to that page in some rulebook, it is more helpful to wonder where an individual or group might position *themselves* along several continuums or within certain categories.

For example, I like to discover the *tendency* for an individual or group in terms of:

- A range of cultural values - do these particular individuals question authority or acquiesce to it? Do they value group consensus over individual aspirations? Do they emphasize cooperation instead of competition?

- A range of behaviors - how do these particular individuals use gestures and what is their sense of personal space? Do they use direct or indirect communication? How do they express affection and disapproval?

- Areas and phases of life - what constitutes good childrearing practices or a formal education or a great marriage? How do these particular individuals handle their money or celebrate their holidays? How much and what kind of leisure do they enjoy?

When you ask questions with these categories and continuums in mind, you can remember how different individuals *within* any culture can be. Within your own family, even if you are 100% from a certain ethnic background, don't you enjoy different leisure activities and have different ideas on the importance of higher education or how emotionally expressive to be?

And, yet, when you compare your kin to a family of a very different background, there are enough similarities in your brood that you can see how you would be thought of as quite unique in comparison to the other family.

What follows are some examples of distinctions between people in terms of what they value, and how they behave. By sharing these true anecdotes of how we approach areas of life differently, I'm hoping you will think about the people in your life and have a better sense of how you might be unwittingly miscommunicating with them or insensitive to what they are trying to express.

PART TWO: MANY DIFFERENT CULTURES

TIME

In some countries (or companies or families), a nine o'clock meeting means to be in your seats at ten minutes to nine or you are already late. In other cultures, showing up by 9:15 is just fine. Our sense of time is one of our most primary orientations in the world. Your way seems so normal and natural (i.e., the true way) that, if someone has a different notion of time, it can feel as if they are disrespecting you. You might think, "They don't value my time."

I remember going to a wedding and showing up about 15 minutes early. I was used to people mingling a bit before the ceremony began. Well, I was the only one there! Everyone else was cued into the fact that the wedding really got started an hour or more after the time on the invitation. A 2 pm wedding really meant "start getting ready for the wedding."

In mainstream U.S. culture, time is strictly linear - the present follows the past; the future follows the present, and so on. Time is an entity that comes from behind you and moves forward. You need to move forward in order to be in step with the "march of time." Lagging behind is unacceptable, so you had better catch up.

For other cultures, time flows toward you from the future. If you are moving slowly, time will wait for you because time isn't a separate and distinct entity - it is something that is continually being created. Whenever you arrive is the exact time for whatever is occurring to be happening.

With such radically different worldviews, it is no wonder that cultural misunderstandings become more prevalent as our society becomes more diverse. Even cultures that have a similar reference to time - seeing time as a spectrum of past, present, and future - can emphasize different ends of that spectrum.

In the dominant culture of the United States, for example, the future is almost a religion. You work for it, dream about it, sacrifice for it, and let it inspire you. The future will inevitably be better.

But for some cultures within the U.S., you will be greeted by blank stares if you try to inspire people by painting a rosy picture of the future ahead. For some, you would be wiser to talk about how career success, test scores, or moral choices "will honor your ancestors and be a credit to your family's past."

You may miss that the person living next door or in the next cubicle or on the other side of your bed is operating on an entirely different idea of the passage of time and its significance.

AUTHORITY

When you look at world events, you can see people's ideas on relating to authority changing in ways that would have been unthinkable only a few years ago. For example, demonstrations in China, Syria, Russia, and Myanmar would have been unheard of!

Years ago, I worked with a woman who had been raised in communist Poland before coming to the United States. Our boss was an open and gregarious leader who consistently prodded us with, "Give me push back here. Tell me where I'm wrong. Speak up!"

One day, this woman cornered me in the women's restroom and whispered, "Is he serious? What happens to those who speak up? Is this his way of getting rid of people?"

It took several years for her to work up the courage *and trust* that it was all right, even helpful, to challenge authority. Today we joke that she never shuts up! She assimilated to the American idea of authority very well. Now, when she visits relatives in Poland, they inevitably comment on how "brash' she's become.

Even in the U.S., there can be a huge gap between people of different generations and different levels of income when it comes to accepting or challenging authority.

At your workplace, do you relate to authority in the context of an unbending hierarchy or as more of an equal and flattened chain of command?

GESTURES

When I was first out of college, I worked on an American Indian reservation, teaching dance movement to high school students as a way to engage kinesthetic learners. I was completely discouraged. No matter how friendly and positive I was, the students seemed absolutely disengaged. They kept looking down at their feet.

Finally, I went to one of the elders and described my frustration. He started to laugh - not exactly the reaction I was expecting. At last, he said to me, "Susan, the students love you! They're just trying to show you respect. You are only a few years older than some of them. They have been taught not to make eye contact with an elder. They are letting you know they accept your authority."

Of course, I was thrilled to be given this very large insight into what was happening with my class. However, I was still confused. "How do I teach them movements, then, if they won't look at me?"

He laughed again. "Turn around, Susan," he said. "Teach your dance steps with your back to the students. Then, come around behind them to watch if they have the correct movement patterns."

Here are a few other examples about gestures that participants in my seminars have shared with me:

- In one department, each time an employee approached her colleague from India, he stood up as a sign of respect. Even if she came into his cubicle 50 times a day, even if he was clearly in the middle of something working on his computer, he always stood up. She felt funny sitting down when he entered her office, but it just wasn't her custom to stand.

- In France, what Americans call the "okay" sign means that something or someone is worthless. It means that they are a zero. In Japan, the same gesture can be the sign for money. In some parts of Germany or in some South American or

Mediterranean countries, the same gesture is obscene. One college student thought she was being positive to her Brazilian dorm mate by signaling that she was in agreement with her roommate's suggestions. How surprised she was to discover that, instead, the roommate felt insulted and quite concerned that she had been assigned that semester to a roommate who could be so lewd.

- In parts of India, rocking the head from side to side doesn't mean, "No." Instead, it means, "Yes, I'm listening." Even a verbal, "Yes" can mean, "I'll consider what you're saying" instead of, "Yes, we have an agreement." Family members and business people alike have walked away thinking they have an agreement, only to find out later that the person who was shaking their head meant no such thing.

ELDER CARE

A colleague of mine worked at an insurance company that sold long-term care insurance to various organizations. (Long-term care insurance is a type of product that covers a stay in a non-hospital, skilled care facility such as a nursing home or rehab center.)

According to the Department of Health and Human Services, 70 percent of folks turning age 65 can expect to be in some form of long-term care facility during their lives. However, regular health insurance, Medicare, and Medicaid only cover 11% of these costs. With people living longer, long-term insurance is gaining in popularity.

However, my colleague's insurance firm was having trouble selling the idea to one organization. The firm's marketing group conducted interviews, focus groups, and other demographic research. They discovered that the employees of this organization were 70% Latino.

When they delved deeper, they found that this mostly Latino employee population was from many different Central and Latin American countries but a common thread seemed to be that they viewed long-term care insurance as an abdication of their valued roles as family caretakers. There was a cultural expectation that younger and healthier family members took care of their sick and elderly relatives. It was assumed that if family members became ill, they would be taken care of by other family members.

Thereafter, the insurance company changed its marketing approach to position long-term care insurance as a complement to a family's very important role. They positioned the family and the nursing facility as partners. The families would still be primarily responsible - any additional care through a nursing facility or a home health aide would just provide technological and staffing expertise that might not be in a family member's home. Any outside facility would be an *extension* of home care.

FAMILY RESPONSIBILITIES

In light of the many ways families can be structured in the U.S., some institutions have had to re-examine their family leave policies. I had one colleague who was so distraught that he almost quit a very satisfying job.

His company allowed employees time off for a funeral for "immediate family." In this man's culture, what some would call a 4th or 5th cousin *was* immediate family to him. In fact, in his culture, it was insulting to call attention to the ranking of cousins and family members as first, second and so forth.

This was a family that gathered every Sunday for a shared meal, and made casual visits to each other's homes at least once or twice during the week. They attended every birth, wedding, birthday and religious holiday together. If it came down to losing his job or attending his cousin's funeral, he knew the choice he had to make.

In academic situations, I've worked with many educators who are frustrated by how some of their students' academic success is limited by family responsibilities. These educators have watched promising students jeopardize an outstanding grade by missing a mid-term exam, for instance, because a family member needed them and family always came first.

Some of these educators have found it helpful to call family conferences where everyone can discuss the balance between short-term responsibilities - helping a cousin with daycare, taking an aunt to a doctor's appointment - and long-term family benefits when a son or daughter successfully completes their education.

WORK/LIFE BALANCE

Some people have culture shock when they come into an American work environment and are expected to work 50, 60, and even 70 hours a week. Perhaps they came from a culture where everyone went home between one and three in the afternoon. They had lunch with their families, and maybe even took a brief nap.

Work/life balance can be greatly influenced by other dimensions of diversity. Age, gender, family issues, and marital status can all affect how Americans balance their work and personal lives. This highlights, once again, the differences *within* cultures.

We certainly see different preferences between generations when it comes to this dimension of work/ life balance. You might hear young people say that they are determined to have a life, to not work all the time as so many of their parents have.

However, work/life balance may mean very different things to different generations. While many older workers seek personal time with no interference from work, many younger workers don't mind blurring life and work. They feel as though they are "having a life" when they can bring their children or pets into work or wear casual clothes.

I once worked with a technology support person who was absolutely marvelous. He didn't mind being interrupted while working out at the gym or practicing his moves at the skateboard park. The important thing for him was that he was living the life he wanted. He was glad to give me as much time as needed to solve any problem as long as he could be out doing the things he loved.

Most younger workers don't expect to give up everything for the company, but that doesn't mean they won't put in long hours when needed. Companies that are willing to be flexible and creative with their workers' delivery methods get larger contributions from them.

BEAUTY

An exchange student from Ethiopia had shown up for a youth group event I was moderating. We were talking over dinner when she complained to me about how rude Americans were.

"Why do you think Americans are rude?" I asked.

"Well, for instance, we went to the swimming pool and five or six girls asked me, 'How do you stay so thin?' I was so shocked and upset, I had to leave."

I explained to the student that, in America, a statement such as, "How do you stay so thin?" isn't a request for information so much as it is a compliment.

However, coming from Ethiopia where plumpness is a desirable physical body type, the girl was insulted by the question.

"They were giving me a compliment?" she responded in disbelief. "No, I do not think so. I am too skinny."

I have to say that I was tempted to be a bit envious of this girl's cultural norms. However, whether a society says you are supposed to be thin or heavy, cultural expectations around beauty can leave many of us feeling uneasy about our bodies.

PUBLIC APPRECIATION

Some Europeans who were new congregants in a Midwestern church were disconcerted by how Americans whistled at large public events. But the real mind-blowing event for them occurred when they heard the congregants break into applause, whoops and whistles after visiting musicians played a hymn at their church!

In many European countries, whistling after a concert means that the audience disapproves of the performance. How could these people - in a church of God! - be so mean to the musicians?

CLEANLINESS

I had a friend who was Japanese American. He had come to the U.S. when he was a teenager and was now quite successful as a Vice President of his company.

We were talking on the phone one evening after I had had a particularly long, grueling day. I remarked, "I am so looking forward to finishing dinner and, then, soaking in the tub."

He remarked, "Do you know how 'dirty' Americans can seem to Japanese people?"

He went on to explain, "When you all take a bath, you clean yourselves in the tub and then soak in that same water! To most Japanese taking a bath that way makes no sense at all. Most Japanese shower and clean themselves first. Then they get into their bath to relax. Many American customs are second nature to me now. But I just can't take a tub bath without showering first."

I have to say I have never thought of my way of taking a bath in same light again.

TAKING TURNS

I was at a post office in a small town in Italy. Several people were crowding around the service window, everyone talking at once. It seemed completely chaotic to me. I thought people were being pushy, loud and aggressive.

I wanted to shout out, "Would everyone take their turn, please?"

When I got back to where I was staying and commented on what I had witnessed, my host family's mother explained. "We find your American way of waiting in line to be quite impractical," she said.

"How can waiting in line be impractical?" I asked.

"If someone is waiting in a post office line," she said, "and they have to fill out a label, everyone behind that person has to wait. In our town, several of us gather around a service window so that many transactions can be going on at once. While you're filling out your label, someone else is paying for his or her purchase."

It was a moment of self-reflection for me: when I didn't understand what was going on, my mind went right to judgment. If I had said or insinuated something in the post office about how "rude" everyone was behaving, I would have been one of those "Ugly Americans."

No harm was done, thank goodness, but sometimes cultural misunderstandings can be downright dangerous...

DIRECT AND INDIRECT COMMUNICATION

One of the most extreme examples of the difference in cultural styles was detailed in Malcolm Gladwell's book *Outliers*. In his chapter "The Ethnic Theory of Plane Crashes," he describes a cross-cultural miscommunication that truly became a matter of life or death.

In researching the crash of the Columbian Avianca Flight 052 on its way to New York's Kennedy Airport in 1990, investigators determined that a difference in cultural communication styles was one of the main causes of the crash.

Before the accident, the New York City Air Traffic Control (ATC) had temporarily re-routed the Columbian jetliner. Here is the actual transcript from the black box *right before the plane crashed*:

> Air Traffic Control (ATC): I'm gonna bring you about fifteen miles northeast and then turn you back onto the approach.

The first officer on the Avianca 052 replied:

> Klotz (first officer): I guess so. Thank you very much.

They are about to crash and the first officer is acquiescing to the ATC's authority with an indirect, *I guess so. Thank you very much*!?!

The first officer never used what we would call direct communication: "This is an emergency! Fuel too low! I cannot execute your command for a fly around. We must land now!"

To the Kennedy Airport Air Traffic Control operators their direct way of communicating is the fastest, most effective way in a constrained environment that handles an exceptional amount of traffic. But to someone not used to this style (in Columbia or, for that matter, in a small town in the U.S.) the New York ATC's typical communication style could be seen as demanding, even threatening.

However, the ATC operators' cultural expectations are that if someone doesn't like what an ATC operator is saying, then *he or she* should give immediate and equally firm feedback, not subtle hints that they are running out of fuel.

We react from our cultural upbringing more than we know. It was nearly impossible for these Columbian flight officers to speak back to the New York ATC's direct commands without first being given permission, training, and practice.

Luckily, most cross-cultural misunderstandings are not life or death situations. However, even a series of slight misunderstandings can build into an impression that you are insensitive and uncaring. Your relationships will suffer.

PART THREE: TRAFFIC LIGHT NEGOTIATIONS

SIDESTEP THE 3R DISEASE

You are who you are; you have been brought up a certain way and you *do* see the world the way you see it. So what can you do to foster better cross-cultural relationships? First, let me tell you what *not* to do.

Do whatever you can to keep from being infected with the 3 R Disease:

1. Resist - "That's crazy!" (also, "weird," "perverted," "stupid," etc.) You make the other person or culture wrong. You can spoil an entire trip by being angry at a whole country and its customs.

2. Resent - "How dare they misunderstand me! Who do they think they are?" You take the differences personally. You feel insulted and close down or cut the other person out of your life.

3. Revenge - "They are wrong and I will make them pay!" People who have been corrected may respond by not sharing valuable information or not inviting someone to social events or even passing someone by for an important assignment or promotion. They feel justified because they feel the other person is "just too hard to work with" when the truth is that they can't acknowledge that they have had a negative effect on someone else.

Deep acceptance of yourself and Both/And thinking is called for in cross-cultural mishaps so that you don't become defensive. You can intend one thing *and* realize that the impact on someone else can be quite different. You can know you are a good person *and* be sorry if you had a negative impact on someone else.

No matter how smart you are, you can't possibly know everything about all the cultures in the world. It's okay not to know *and* you can actually enjoy learning as much as you can.

When you feel confident in yourself, it's easier to be open to other people's feedback. You understand that you can flex your style without giving up your values or who you are. You can face other people's discontent without getting defensive and instead be grateful to learn.

When you are open to other people's worldview and feedback, you won't be the "Ugly American" - complaining, barking orders and walking away in a huff.

So how do you do all this?

MOVE UNDERSTANDING INTO ACTION

You've already taken action by reading this book. Greater awareness of the differences between and within cultures is the first stage.

Next, I recommend a simple, three-step process to avoid cultural clashes. Since many of you are traveling abroad or moving about this country or even across town to other cultures, let's use the red, yellow and green of a Traffic Light for our guide. The first step in avoiding cultural collisions is to Stop! and question the assumptions you are making. Then, you need to Wait! so that you can slow down to learn as much as you can about the cultures with which you will be or are interacting. Finally, you will need to Go! into action to make a decision or to negotiate "how we'll do things here."

THE CULTURAL TRAFFIC LIGHT

Stop!
Withhold judgment

Wait!
Slow down and seek understanding of each other's cultures

Go!
Decide whose norms to follow, compromise or create a new possibility

STEP ONE: STOP - WITHHOLD JUDGEMENT

As you learn about how differently people approach the cultural aspects of living, you can start to appreciate the wide variety of packages in which we human beings come.

How would you be the same and how would you be different if you had been raised in a different culture? How much of the way you see the world is because of a social norm and how much is specific to your individual personality or values?

Understanding the arbitrariness of your own identity can keep you from forming an instant negative opinion of those who are different from you.

Keep in mind that, to others, their actions are normal. To avoid the trap of a judgmental mind, remember that you always have the choice of being right or being happy. Choosing the route of open-mindedness and living in peace with others doesn't mean you have to "dumb-down" your values and accept every aspect of another culture. It means understanding that the ways of others make sense to them and were fashioned for the same reasons that your own cultural customs were created - for security, for social cohesion, for ease of social interactions, and the like.

Everyone acts in the ways that, to them, seem logical.

Most people don't need your absolute agreement to work well with you. Even when there's disagreement, you can still have a productive relationship when everyone feels seen, respected, and appreciated.

A colleague of mine who is an academic advisor at a community college was frustrated that some of her female students came to registration and other educational conferences with their husbands, uncles, or brothers who did most of the talking. Raised in the post-feminist West, the advisor found this custom of male chaperoning outdated and even oppressive.

Eventually, she became friendly with one of these women. The woman explained to her advisor that knowing that her male relatives "had her back" allowed her the mental freedom to focus fully on her studies.

The advisor still needed to explain the cultural norms of the school - at which times the teachers and administrators would need the woman to express *her* solo desires and opinions - but the advisor started to see through the eyes of that student's cultural lens.

While not the gender roles she wanted to live by, my colleague began to accept that certain kinds of male chaperoning could be seen as freeing rather than limiting to those of another culture.

Removing her harsh judgments made it easier for this advisor to relate to the many different kinds of adult students who attended her community college. She said her biases were almost like "wearing headsets or blinders" when her students and their families came to see her. She realized that she was so put off by her interpretation of some of their cultural customs that she was missing much of what they were saying to her.

LET YOUR MORE EVOLVED BRAIN BE IN CHARGE

Our tendency to make snap judgments goes back to the age of early humans. You can see why human beings had a major preoccupation with safety. We'd constantly scan the horizon for trouble. If trouble came, we had to make split-second decisions - fight or flight. If a saber tooth tiger came leaping out of the bush we didn't ask, "Now, what kind of childhood did he have to make him so nasty?" No! We reacted from the survival part of our brain. It was fight or flight. Either/Or. Life or death.

Let's call that survival brain our Old Brain. That older, survival part of our brain is dualistic. It doesn't have time for complex reasoning. It keeps things simple: Right/wrong. Good/ bad. My group/their group. Us/them.

Our Old Brain is making judgments all the time. It's hyper alert! Truly, if electrodes were hooked up to your brain when you are afraid, the oldest part of your brain, your hypothalamus, the part of your brain at the back and bottom of your skull, would be firing away.

Old Brain might have been our protection in old days, but, now, (when we are not in danger) we have to move beyond it and come from New Brain. When we are in the more evolved part of our brain, we have choice. The frontal lobe, the larger part of our brain, is firing away when we are thinking things through and making decisions. We are actually more secure and protected when we are making reasoned choices.

But Old Brain will fight for control. It will be screaming, "Watch out! He's... (fill in the blank with judgments and assumptions)." You want to listen to that part of your brain - there *may* be danger - but you do not want Old Brain running the show. Listen to the warnings and judgments and then consciously move into New Brain where you can make cogent decisions.

It's a blessing that we have a part of us, like an inner alarm, that goes off when we are seeing something that seems out of the ordinary or possibly menacing. You just don't want that survival part of your brain, Old Brain, in charge.

Realize that Old Brain sees enemies everywhere. Your New Brain can more accurately decide if something is a threat or not.

So first hear your assumptions. You have to consciously choose to be aware of them. Sometimes, they are so unconscious you'll protest, "But I don't have any biases!" If that's true, you may be the only human alive who is bias-free.

The problem isn't in having biases, it is in being unaware of them. You can't change something if you don't even know it's there. When you are conscious of the judgments subtly zipping through your mind, you can challenge and manage them.

STEP TWO: WAIT - SEEK UNDERSTANDING

Before you tour another country, visit a particular part of this country or go to a business or family event in a different cultural environment, be proactive. Read about that culture. Go to cultural events such as film festivals, lectures and holiday celebrations.

But be cautious. The older part of your brain, your survival brain, wants it easy. It loves to label. When your Old Brain is running the show, you can be immersed in a culture that has lots of variety and only see the people as "them," one homogenous group.

Remember no single culture is just one thing. Seek out and become aware of multiple points of view within the same culture while recognizing the culture's unique tendencies and similarities.

Ask yourself, "What is my cultural lens? What might I be misinterpreting here?"

If you have any allies from that same culture, ask them, "What do you see as some of the biggest mistakes others have made at your family (business or community) events? What do you wish others understood about your culture?" and "What reads as respect or disrespect?"

Let them know you are open to feedback: "I want to be considerate. Would you be willing to tell me if I do something that comes across as insensitive?"

Slow down enough to take your cues from the locals. If you arrive at someone's home and you see that everyone has removed his or her shoes, you have been given a very big clue as to a cultural custom in this house. If you are greeted with someone's extended hand (as opposed to a hug, a bow or a nod of the head), they have shared their cultural expectations with you.

You won't always know if the disparities between you and other people come from your nationalities, your ethnic groups, your professions or the peculiarities of your families and personalities. However, no matter the source, one of the best things you can do is to talk about possible areas of misunderstanding *before* you are in the heat of the moment.

The "Hofstede's Dimensions" mentioned in the jetliner crash story can help you. Here are a baker's dozen of different cultural continuums. These will offer a great start for you to sit down with someone and increase your understanding of one another.

Or, as a group exercise, individuals in departments, committees, teams or even families can rate themselves. Each individual asks, "Where do I fall on this continuum?"

To make the group variations visible, you can put these continuums on a flipchart or white board. Each participant gets a different set of colored adhesive dots. Have participants put the adhesive dots where they feel they would fall on each continuum. That way, you can get a visual picture of the tendencies and differences within your group.

CULTURAL VALUES

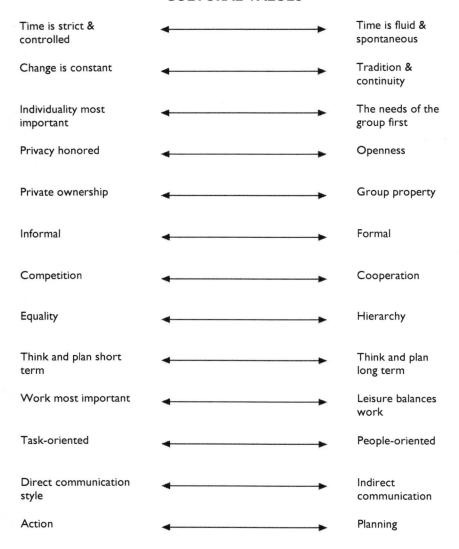

Time is strict & controlled	Time is fluid & spontaneous
Change is constant	Tradition & continuity
Individuality most important	The needs of the group first
Privacy honored	Openness
Private ownership	Group property
Informal	Formal
Competition	Cooperation
Equality	Hierarchy
Think and plan short term	Think and plan long term
Work most important	Leisure balances work
Task-oriented	People-oriented
Direct communication style	Indirect communication
Action	Planning

Cultural values I might misunderstand or around which I might feel uncomfortable:

Cultures about which I know the least or with which I have less experience:

(For a free copy of the Cultural Continuum poster, go to: www.SusanOHalloran.com)

Had the Columbian and New York airline employees - specifically the flight crews and ATC operators - done this exercise, they may have seen the vast differences between each group in relationship to authority and communication styles.

PREVENT CONFLICTS
BEFORE THEY BEGIN

By taking the time to look at similarities and differences, individuals and organizations can begin to understand:

- where potential or existing misunderstandings lie
- if any member of a family or team is working at cross purposes with the rest of the group
- if a cultural norm needs to be changed
- where decisions need to be made

If you practice this preventive communication, you can flex your style to work well with others or, if one style needs to prevail in a given situation, everyone understands that beforehand.

STEP THREE: GO - DECIDE WHOSE CULTURAL NORMS TO FOLLOW

You can imagine how well-received a boss is who barks, "You're in America now - do it our way!"

To the other extreme, in trying to reach out to and understand other cultures, this doesn't mean we throw up our hands and say, "Well, I have to be culturally sensitive so we'll just have to do things their way!" If you try to be "understanding" in this way, the resentments will pile up until you are ready to blow!

Just as sports teams have to have someone calling the plays from time to time, there are times when people in authority (or a group of people) need to make the decision, "This is how we do things here, right now."

The Avianca Flight 052 tragedy was a wake-up call. The airline industry realized that they needed to train their flight officers to consider themselves equal to Air Traffic Controllers and each other. To create a new "This is how we do things here," a number of airline companies insisted, for example, that airline captains, first officers and ATC operators call each other by their first names.

Further, flight officers (of every nationality) were taught to replace indirect, moderating communication with a standardized direct communication procedure where copilots, for example, were encouraged to challenge captains.

If a copilot thought that something was amiss, he or she was instructed to say, "I'm concerned...", and "I'm uncomfortable with...", and even "I believe this situation is unsafe."

Gladwell states: "Aviation experts will tell you that it is the success of this war on mitigating communication as much as anything else that accounts for the extraordinary decline in airline accidents in recent years."

In this case, the cultural norm of a more direct communication style was negotiated, decided, and implemented. It was determined that direct communication worked best in emergency situations and is now part of the airline culture's "this is how we do things here."

In other situations, you can negotiate a compromise or a unique hybrid of your different cultural norms.

SO HOW DO YOU NEGOTIATE?

Negotiating means finding a way forward that both of you can live with. Growing up, most of us saw models of passivity: withdrawing, sugarcoating, couching, selective truth telling and giving in. You hurt yourself.

Or people taught us to get our way through aggression: belittling, overpowering, manipulating, threatening, interrupting, name-calling and being sarcastic. You hurt others.

Being assertive, on the other hand, means communicating without hurting yourself or hurting others. When you negotiate without hurting yourself or anyone else, both people's integrity and power stay intact.

Think of this Third Step - Go! - as happening in three stages:

A. Reassure each other that everyone can get what they want
B. Find the wants below the wants and try on the other person's perspective
C. Find common ground and/or make a mutually agreed-upon decision

FIND THE WANTS BELOW THE WANTS

People often fight out of a feeling of scarcity. If someone tends to be more aggressive, they can think, "If you win, I lose so I better make sure I come out on top." Or if someone is more passive and has a script such as, "Don't make waves," they will give up and give in. However, over time, their bitterness grows.

To avoid the extremes of aggression or passivity, reassure yourself and the person with whom you are in conflict. Tell them, " I want to find a solution we both can feel good about. I'm sure there are creative, cooperative solutions that will work for both of us."

Next, define the problem. Make sure that you are both having the same conversation. Ask yourself honestly, "Is what we are arguing over what I am really upset about? What else might it be?"

You think you are arguing about a cultural custom, but when you are honest with yourself you realize you are jealous that someone else got the promotion you wanted. You think someone has disrespected you by saying you were insensitive, but you realize you are really embarrassed that this person knows you have made a mistake. We're often not upset for the reasons we think we are.

The next part of this stage is the most crucial: When you have defined the problem, let go of the form, the exact way you think the solution has to look. Search for the deeper wants. Ask each other, "What will you get by having…?"

Let's take a non-cultural example: a decision many friends or couples make each year – where to vacation.

I want a trip to the ocean; you want to go to the mountains.

If both of us hold fast to the exact form – ocean or mountains – there will be no common ground.

However, when you ask me, "What do you get by going to the ocean?" the conversation starts to shift.

I tell you that being by water calms me. I love the sound of the water and the sun on my face.

Then, I ask you, "What will you get by having a vacation in the mountains?"

You answer, "I love the crisp air, the breeze, the smell of pine trees and walks in the woods."

We repeat each other's wants to our satisfaction. Yes! I understand your desires and you understand mine. "Thank you for telling me. I'd like to support you in getting what you want." (I keep reminding myself with positive self-talk that if you get what you want, it doesn't mean I won't get what I want.)

Now we brainstorm options that encompass both of our points of view or we create a new point of view together. What ideas can fulfill our deepest desires below our initial wants? When we uncover our deepest desires, we begin to see that there is more than one way to satisfy our needs.

For example, maybe you and I decide to vacation at a lake with a waterfall next to a forest. I get the sound of running water and you get your walk in the woods. By letting go of the exact form, we find a trip that makes both of us happy.

CONSCIOUS DECISIONS

Of course, sometimes making a conscious cultural choice can mean that one end or another of a cultural continuum will dominate. But this choice can be accepted by a wide variety of people when there has been discussion - people feel heard - and the reasoning is understood. The choice is presented as "This is the way that works best for this particular time and situation," as opposed to "This is the right and only way. I'm right and you're wrong!"

Hundreds of years of histories, differing political structures, religious traditions, artistic contributions, linguistic expressions, and so forth can still be honored even when a choice for one end of a cultural scale is chosen over another.

Whatever cultural norms dominate, there are always ways of providing touchstones of familiarity for different cultures at least part of the time. Even formal work environments, for example, have casual dress days. Even families with the strictest of guidelines on bedtimes for young children bend the rules on certain occasions.

Negotiating "whose standards and customs, when?" can take time, but ultimately this kind of flexibility saves time. *We pay now or we pay later.* Put in the effort *before* conflicts arise or spend your energy dealing with the consequences of your misunderstandings and hard feelings.

What is interesting is how, when we *consciously* decide a cultural norm, others for whom the change was not initially made benefit as well.

At a community college where I taught, students in non-mainstream religions were faced with observing their holy days or taking important tests. When the college began moving more of their testing to online and gave students the ability to take tests within a time period of several days, students from all religious and non-religious backgrounds remarked how the flexibility benefited them.

In a previous example - for my friend who wanted to attend his cousin's funeral - when the company eventually changed their family leave policies, a company survey revealed that workers from varied backgrounds pointed out the more flexible family leave policy as one of their reasons for job satisfaction and loyalty to their company.

In both these examples, at the college and in the workplace, people got to the third step of negotiation - Go! - and:

A. Reassured each other that everyone could get what they wanted
B. Found the wants below the wants and tried on the other person's perspective
C. Found common ground and made a mutually agreed-upon decision

WHEN *NOT* TO NEGOTIATE

At times you won't want to have a discussion about whose way will prevail. When you are in Great Britain you are not going to have a debate about which side of the road to drive on. You'll drive like everyone else: "When in Rome..." and all that.

At other times, you won't want to negotiate because your values or your discomfort trumps the cultural norm.

For example, a woman in one of my seminars shared that she had gone to Germany during the summer when she was a freshmen in college. She had become friendly in high school with an exchange student from Germany. In college, her parents allowed her to go to Germany for a month to visit her high school friend and her family.

"What a shock!" she said. "When I met my friend's parents at the airport for the first time, they both gave me a hug and then kissed me on the lips!"

The woman's own family was famous for their air hugs. "We barely touched in my family!" she explained. "And here were these two strangers kissing me on the lips!"

Of course, there are German families that don't kiss on the lips and American families from all ethnic backgrounds that do. It doesn't really matter where the custom originates from if you are uncomfortable with it.

It would have been perfectly fine for this young woman to tell her host family that she preferred to hug and kiss on the cheek (or not at all). As a college student, she didn't know how to be that upfront in expressing her preferences, but she said, "Eventually, I guess they got the idea as I kept turning my head away from their kisses."

Also, when she went to the beach with this German family, the mother and father as well as many other people on the beach, changed in and out of their swimming suits right in the open.

"There would be the Dad," she shared, "eating a sandwich, in his birthday suit, talking away as if nothing out of the ordinary was happening!"

Again, while it would be useless to judge and condemn everyone on the beach, this young woman is perfectly in her rights to explain that she won't be changing her clothes in front of everyone and that she means no disrespect by turning her eyes away when other people do.

BE OPEN *AND* BE YOU

Being open to other people's cultural expression does not mean compromising your values. It means you understand that others do what they do because it makes sense to them, not because they are "weird" or "strange."

In other words, when you set limits with a "This is simply me" energy (as opposed to a judgmental attitude and tone of voice that says, "What's wrong with you?") most people will accept your personal standards.

If they argue with you or make fun of you, that is their problem. Stay calm and firm.

While there is little you can do about the cultural norms for negotiating space, for example, when you are packed into a crowded subway in New York, Tokyo or Mexico City, you *can* explain your need for a certain amount of distance between you and another person when you are talking one on one.

PART FOUR: RESOLVING CULTURAL CLASHES

AND IF THERE IS A MISUNDERSTANDING

When there has been a mistake or a misunderstanding, instead of thinking a terrible thing has happened, start thinking that the *expected* thing has happened. With so many different cultures coming together in our organizations, communities and homes, we're bound to have misunderstandings and conflicts.

Some of us avoid conflict at all costs. We smell trouble coming and we run the other way. Our mantra becomes: "Make no waves!"

Others of us go immediately into "dukes up." We are ready to fight!

Whether we see conflict as a threat or an attack, many of us go into a flight or fight stress response. At that moment it can feel as though you are fighting or fleeing for your life. However, every one of us can remember events in our lives that, at the time, seemed like the absolute worst possible thing to happen and, later, it turned out to be one of the best.

We never know what gift is contained in a conflict or misunderstanding. That sounds like Pollyanna talk, but it really is how life works. Every novelist, scriptwriter, and playwright knows this: the challenges of life and the rewards are always sown together.

At least think of it this way: it is better if someone lets *you* know they have a problem with something you are doing rather than telling everyone else. We all have blind spots when it comes to other people's cultures. Most of us would rather learn in easy and joyful ways but, sometimes, the only way we can become aware that we are doing something insensitive or inappropriate is when we step on someone else's toes and they yell, "Ouch!"

Out of habit while in Bali, Indonesia, I unconsciously patted a toddler on the head. I was feeling great affection for the family with whom I was visiting. They had set out fruits for me, and had all taken a break from their daily activities so that we could talk. I had been warned that this gesture could be seen as offensive but, again, I forgot and did it automatically.

My host, the child's mother, pulled me aside and told me that the head is considered sacred in most parts of Indonesia and should never be touched. I apologized to her family and thanked her for informing me. "I'm sorry" or "Forgive me" are two of your most important words in your cross-cultural vocabulary.

The woman and I became friendly for the rest of my visit to her village. She told me later that she had explained this custom to others in the past and all of them immediately defended themselves with, "I didn't mean anything!" The intent (what I meant by the gesture) was very different than the impact (how threatened the child and family felt by my patting him on the head).

Always acknowledge the impact first.

It's natural to want to defend yourself, but it's much appreciated by others when you simply listen and take in the information they are offering.

THE L-I-V-E FORMULA

If someone comes to you with a complaint about something you said or did and they are A-N-G-R-Y, not just pointing out your mistake, but truly upset, don't get defensive and don't panic.

You will LIVE through this confrontation when you use the L-I-V-E FORMULA:

 lean in and listen

 investigate and show your intention to understand

 vision together - what are the possible options or solutions?

 have clear expectations - what are your agreements and next steps?

STEP ONE: L = LEAN IN AND LISTEN

When someone comes to you with a complaint about something you said or did and is very emotional, buy yourself some time. Memorize this phrase:

"Tell me more about that."

Yes! Although you want to run the other way or blast back at them, actually invite them to talk more.

You are giving yourself a chance to come from a calm, centered place within. As they talk, you can give yourself some quick, internal, supportive self-talk:

- "Okay, I can handle this. Take a breath."

- "This could be good. There has been tension between us. We can finally clear the air."

- "She respects me enough to say this to my face."

- "Calm down. No need to get mad back. This is just his way of expressing himself right now. He is telling me about what is important to him."

If you will take several slow breaths as you listen to the other person vent, you can break your nervous system's emergency signal that starts to race through your body when you hear criticism.

When Old Brain gets a signal of "Emergency!" remember it will react as if the situation is life or death *and* very personal. However, your Old Brain's defensive responses - fight, flight, freeze or faint - won't be helpful in this situation.

BRING THEM BACK TO BALANCE

Encourage people who are upset with you to express their feelings and values. As you breathe and resist taking their comments personally, let them tell you why they are so upset.

First of all, when you lean in and listen, you will surprise them because they, all of us, are so rarely listened to and second, once people feel they are being received they often return to some balance. Sometimes, they will actually start to defend *you*: "Well, I don't mean you 'always' do this. Sometimes, you have been very sensitive, of course."

As they vent, echo back in the form of a question what you are hearing, "So letting the elder in your family speak first is really important to you?"

As you hear them and empathize with their frustration, they will start to wind down. You (and they) will start to understand what is really bothering them. If you have done something to upset them, the issue will become more specific and, therefore, manageable once they have let off steam.

People often think they have to build up their case to feel justified in being upset. Often, just letting someone have a "Vesuvius moment" (spewing all the venom) will bring the issue down to size.

Like my Balinese friend, the other person expects to hear an argument: "But I didn't mean anything!" When you actually listen to someone else, strong emotions subside and the learning can begin.

So, again, memorize these words - "Tell me more about that" - so that if someone comes to you upset about a cultural faux pas, the words are there. When you go into listening mode, your relationship stays intact and can return to harmony and, sometimes, even deepen because of your increased understanding.

STEP TWO: I = INVESTIGATE, SHOW YOUR INTENTION TO UNDERSTAND

Once the other person has had their "Vesuvius moment" - you will visibly see them calming down - show your desire to understand their concern by asking *investigative* questions such as:

- "What is there about your culture's history that I am not understanding?"
- "What is the meaning behind that gesture?"
- "What did my insensitivity remind you of? When have you faced this before?"

Throughout, keep stating your *intention* that everything works out between the two of you. Say:

- "I really want a positive outcome to this situation."
- "I'd really like to handle this issue to both our satisfaction."
- "I'd love to see us reach an understanding."
- "I want you to feel like you are being heard."
- "I'm committed to working this out."
- "I want you to feel understood and respected."

Check throughout that you are understanding. You *show* your intention to understand by paraphrasing. Sincerely speak phrases such as:

- "What I hear you saying is… Do I have it right?"
- "Let me know if I am on track. You're saying… Am I understanding you?"
- "When you say ___ do you mean ___ or _____?"
- "It seems you need… Is that correct?"

And don't forget to use two of the most important words in your diversity toolbox, "Forgive me…"

"I hope that you can forgive me" is more active than saying, "I'm sorry." You are involving them and giving them control by acknowledging that it's up to them to forgive you.

If you do give an apology, don't follow it with a bunch of excuses. This is *their* time to talk and be understood. *Later,* if your intention is for clearer understanding (not to be right, to put them down or to get back at them), you can ask that they listen to your perspective.

STEP THREE: V = VISION TOGETHER

When it seems that they have vented - you understand the situation and they feel understood - request their desired outcome. Ask:

- "What is most important to you here?"
- "What would make you feel this situation has been handled?"
- "What does it look like when this problem is solved?"
- "What would you need to see or hear from me to know you have been fully understood?"
- "What would be a satisfying outcome for you?"
- "Before we started this conversation, you felt _____. What can I do to change that feeling to a feeling of confidence that this issue is resolved?"
- "How can we rebuild the trust between us?"

In Step Three, the visioning step, you are facing the challenge together rather than being at odds. You are guiding the person's neural activity to move from their Old Brain to their New Brain, the place of possibilities and choices.

STEP FOUR: E = HAVE CLEAR EXPECTATIONS

End the conversation, making sure the two of you have clear expectations and agree on your next steps. Ask:

- "So we've agreed that our next steps are..."
- "If you were in charge of making sure that what you desired truly happened, what would you want to happen next?"
- "Will that work for you?"
- "Here is what I'm willing to do..."
- "Would you be willing to...?" (If they answer "No" ask, "Then what would you be willing to do?")
- "I need to know you won't hold this against me; that you hear my intent to work on this blind spot and to create a mutually rewarding relationship. Do we have that understanding?" (If they answer "No" ask, "What else do I need to do to rebuild trust?")
- "Let's get back on (date) and check in to see that we are proceeding according to our plan."

WHEN YOU USE THE L-I-V-E FORMULA*, REMEMBER TO...

- Show appreciation - it is better to know what someone thinks than have people talking behind your back

- Don't take the feedback personally but do act responsibly. The person with the complaint is telling you lots about him or herself (what they want, don't like, things that previously happened to them) and *perhaps* something you may need to change. Be responsible in making the appropriate changes, but remember that their comments are *never* about your importance or worth as a person. One interaction or even several interactions do not define you.

- Paraphrase throughout for clear understanding. Restate and SHOW your intention to truly understand them.

- Consider the feedback as growth. You may have to direct them to a more respectful communication with you *later*. After they have had their say and feel fully heard, let them know how they can best approach you in the future.

- Clarify and confirm expectations. Agree on the next steps.

- Keep all of your agreements and, if anything changes, let them know and re-negotiate to both your satisfaction.

---

* Based on the work of Bea Young Associates www.BeaYoung.com, Perrone-Ambrose Associates www.Perrone-Ambrose.com and O'Halloran Diversity Productions. For a free copy of the L-I-V-E Formula poster, go to: www.SusanOHalloran.com

TIMING IS EVERYTHING

Again, perhaps later, you may need to teach other people a better way to communicate with you. You could say something such as:

> *"I am so glad you came to me and told me what was bothering you the other day. I know that took a lot of courage to share what's on your mind.*
>
> *I wanted to let you know that what really works for me is when you tell me how you feel and what you want. Please come to me any time you have a concern and I will ask you in the future not to use adjectives to describe me such as "insensitive" or "arrogant" or phrases such as "You never" and "You always." I don't want to get defensive and miss, in any way, the important feedback you have for me.*
>
> *How does that sound to you? I would love to have an agreement that if either of us is upset about anything the other person says or does, we will discuss those behaviors and not make remarks about each other's character? Does that work for you?*
>
> *I really like working with you on this project and want our communication to be as clear and as friendly as possible."*

Use the words that fit your style and personality, but do check that you aren't unwittingly blaming them or telling them what they "should" do.

LISTEN FIRST

In a nutshell, the L-I-V-E Formula asks you to listen to the other person first. Even if they are dead wrong, DO NOT try to explain yourself at that moment. You will only make them more upset. This is why you need to think about and practice receiving feedback *ahead of time*. When you have two reactive people, you get nowhere.

Be the bigger person. **L**isten first. Then truly empathize and **I**nvestigate their concerns in a non-blaming and non-judgmental way. Move them out of fight or flight, the survival part of their Old Brain, into their frontal, more balance cortex of the New Brain. Guide them to en**V**ision the solution and feel hopeful and even enthusiastic about things working out. End the conversation with clear **E**xpectations about your next steps.

It's a challenge not to make the other person wrong, to just let their cynicism or complaints be. However, if you negatively resist their feedback, you make it more real. Just let them be and put your focus on generating possibilities. People get moved that you keep going:

- "You are right. It could be a challenge and I'm committed to..."
- "Yes, it won't be perfect and I'm committed to..."
- "You're right. I make a lot of mistakes and I'm committed to..."

You are not looking for a victory here but a win/win. You give up being right, a very short-lived victory, and realize that the only true "win" is when your relationship is back in accord.

Put your relationships ahead of your ego and you will receive very few complaints to begin with if you continually use the *preventive* guide we discussed earlier. To avoid cultural collisions, use...

THE CULTURAL TRAFFIC LIGHT

Stop!
Withhold judgment

Wait!
Slow down and seek understanding of each other's cultures

Go!
Decide whose norms to follow, compromise or create a new possibility

WHEN YOU NEED HELP

However, if someone is regularly abusive, constantly complaining, objecting to most everything you do or say, then we are talking about a whole other category of challenge. You may need the intervention of a professional to know how or whether to relate to this person.

Relationships with superiors, co-workers, neighbors and family members are hard enough. When you add cultural differences to the mix, it may take the skilled support of a counselor or mediator to navigate the complex waters of feelings, customs and meaning.

WHAT IF SOMEONE OFFENDS YOU? CAN YOU BE FORGIVING?

It may be hard to realize that some people don't know your cultural norms. They seem so natural to you. Therein, lies the danger. It's as if your norms are the only norms. They seem so, well, normal.

If you are in the majority, everything around you supports this idea that your way is the way "real" human beings behave. Anyone else is the odd person out.

Rarely do we say, "Oh, we each have unique cultural references; let me explain the cultural nuances around here to you." No, unless you are aware, you are more likely to label the one who goes against your habits and customs as bad-mannered, thoughtless, lazy or just plain ignorant.

However, the rules of the game are not so obvious to someone who comes into a new culture.

Truly understanding each dimension of diversity - ethnicity, gender, age, physical abilities, geographic regions, departmental protocol and such - takes time. Cross-cultural communication is a dual action of explaining to newcomers what the culture views as successful behavior while being open to improvements that can come from adopting some of the newcomers' ways.

When you understand all the cultural mistakes you can make, you can be more understanding when someone unintentionally does something that offends you.

PART FIVE: BENEFITS TO ALL

ADVANTAGES BEYOND THE EXPECTED

Hurt or angry feelings from cross-cultural mistakes are unpleasant enough, but they can have other consequences as you travel or as you work and relate to others at home such as:

- higher costs
- time-wasting turnovers
- low productivity
- lack of teamwork
- missed deadlines and delays
- miserable morale
- a negative reputation that affects recruitment, community goodwill or, if you're traveling, your next place to stay
- mistrust between groups such as the police, politicians and the community
- legal and other troubles with those in authority
- strained and even broken relationships
- children and adults who feel caught between cultures, as if they don't belong anywhere

Conversely, clear communication is always the key to turning negatives into positives, whether the clashing norms are coming from society, organizations, family, or just our unique personalities and preferences. Cross-cultural understanding and communication can result in such benefits as:

- greater retention, lower re-training costs
- increased productivity
- superior teamwork
- dependable deliverables
- high morale
- stellar reputation
- trust, innovation and the ability to solve problems together
- harmonious relationships
- and, yes, fun and smooth traveling at home and abroad!

GREATER SKILLS FOR EVERYONE

I have been honored to organize several international panel discussions in corporate and community settings. People who were raised outside the U.S. describe just how unique and confusing American values, customs, and behaviors can be. The audience empathizes and there is always much laughter throughout.

Through these shared stories, the audience members are able to see themselves through a different lens. They get it: U.S. cultural norms are just one set of standards. There are many ways to think and behave in this world and many of the customs described by the panelists, such as more time with family or less emphasis on material goods, were envied by the native U.S. audience members.

Of course, these panels also gave rise to discussions on how extremely different cultures *within* the U.S. can be. Employees from other countries who have been re-located to diverse parts of the United States, for example, often comment on how many different Americas they have experienced.

Having a greater awareness of and appreciation for the many cultures surrounding you - in the U.S. and around the world - isn't just a "nice to have."

Valuing each other is a "must have" for your family, your neighborhood, your workplace, your place of worship, your community and your country.

By resisting each other we won't do a very good job of sharing this planet. We all need to increase our skills in navigating our differences.

GRATEFUL FOR FRIENDSHIP

Count on it: you will experience cultural collisions from time to time. Sometimes, you will run into others in the same way ships have run into icebergs because you won't know what's below the waterline. As you get to know the people with whom you study, live, and work - as you see beneath the surface to understand others better - you can avoid some of these collisions and direct the course of your relationships back to more enjoyable and purposeful interaction.

There is a vast magnificence to living confidently in a multi-cultural world. In many ways, it's not even a matter of choice anymore. Many of us find ourselves living, socializing, worshipping, and working with people with whom we had little to no contact in earlier parts of our lives.

In taking the time to learn about other points of views and learning to talk about, negotiate with, and benefit from differences, you are better prepared to create your own success in this growingly diverse world.

Just the other evening, I sat for hours around a friend's dining room table with our friends who are Christian, Jewish and Muslim, Asian, white, black and brown. We freely asked questions of each other: "Do you cover your head in your own house?" "Why do you bury the body so quickly?" "How is it that in Japan the gesture we use to say 'good-bye' means 'come here'?"

The conversation flowed with great ease and hilarity and even a few tears as loved ones who have passed were remembered. We told stories of our growing up - how we teased younger brothers and sisters, or when we burnt a holiday dinner or how we learned, or didn't learn, to handle money. Every moment we were discovering how we were similar and how we were different. I felt so lucky to be in the company of such great diversity and warmth.

I cherish my family and the homogenous community in which I grew up. However, living in the world of today, in this global community where you don't have to leave your neighborhood to experience hundreds of other cultures, has brought a richness to my life that I could never have imagined as an Irish American girl growing up on the South Side of Chicago.

I hope you are able to experience the same abundance of friendships and colleague-ship. Opening your perspectives will not only make the world a more peaceful place, it will give you permission to express more parts of yourself.

Being aware and accepting of other people's depth and complexity will give you an even greater appreciation for the marvel that is you.

ABOUT US...

Congratulations on taking the time to expand your own cultural competency. At O'Halloran Diversity Productions we are dedicated to building cultural bridges and helping people learn more about each other in guilt-free, practical, and FUN ways.

Please stay in touch through our website and blog at **http://www.SusanOHalloran.com** to hear about upcoming reports, webinars, live seminars, performances and presentations that will help you gain more skills to live confidently in our multi-cultural world.

Whatever your desire - business success, student achievement, congregational integrity, civic unity - increasing your comfort and skill with other cultures will help you reach your goals faster with greater harmony and satisfaction.

There *is* a way to build better relationships and more effective teams plus change the landscape of cultural understanding and skills for your organization.

At O'Halloran Diversity Productions, we have created an extended program that is focused on significantly reducing or eliminating:

- Opposition to change

- Fear of talking about difficult subjects such as race

- Insensitive remarks and behaviors by otherwise "nice" people

- PR nightmares from "incidents"

- The possibility of harassment and discrimination suits

These problems will not be solely solved with one-day workshops and keynotes. One-time events are wonderful, but cannot be expected to offset the stereotypes and cultural misinformation we are bombarded with everyday. We are here to help you and your organization create true transformation.

Other books by Susan O'Halloran:

Non-fiction

Diversity Is All Around Us In Our Schools - Isn't It Time We Get It Right?

Compelling Stories, Compelling Causes: Non Profit Marketing Success

Memories of the Future: Tales From A White Chicago Girlhood

Fiction

The Woman Who Lost Her Heart

The Woman Who Found Her Voice

Storybook Marriage

Peace & Justice Storytelling by Susan O'Halloran:
http://bit.ly/SueOHyoutube

Co-producer of Social Justice Storytelling Videos by Professional Storytellers: **http://www.RaceBridgesStudio.com**

THANK YOU!

Dear family, friends, and fellow and sister colleagues, your support has made all the difference! Thank you, thank you, thank you!

Plus, so much gratitude to the several diversity firms and the thousands upon thousands of clients I have worked with over the years. Your participation and feedback shaped the ideas in this book.

Special thanks to Barbara Levie for her skillful editing, Anne Shimojima for her fine-tuning, and Kristine Maveus-Evenson for the layout of this book and her creative cover design.

> *This book is dedicated to my wonderful clients; you are truly making this world a better place!*

9810423R00052

Printed in Germany
by Amazon Distribution
GmbH, Leipzig